WRITE YOUR BOOK

PUBLISH YOUR BOOK

PROMOTE YOUR BOOK

Corinne Edwards

This book is dedicated

to authors everywhere

who have a book inside

aching to be written.

INTRODUCTION

When I was doing publicity for my books, I met many people at book signings, on television and radio shows – and believe it not, on the street or in a supermarket who told me the same thing.

"As soon as I have time – or when I retire, I am going to write a book. I have an idea that I think is very interesting."

I always had the same answer for them. "Nobody has time. If you want to be a writer I have a one word for you. Write." They always looked at me a little doubtfully and it occurred to me that people just don't know where to start.

Starting is the hardest part. But, you have already started if you have an idea. Books are never written overnight. They develop as they go along. You could almost liken it to taking a whole steak and trying to swallow it. You have to cut it piece by piece to eat it. By the time you are finished, you have had dinner.

The other objection is that the starting has to be perfect. Every word, every punctuation mark. Most authors will tell you that you should not edit a book until it is finished. You are not going to be ready to show your new baby to the world until you give birth so the beginning is to write it for yourself.

ARE YOU READY? LET'S GET GOING

CHAPTER ONE – GETTING STARTED

Most books, except for novels have an introduction. So, the first step is to go to your computer and write what your book is about. Or, if you write like I do, I start with a yellow pad of paper.

The next part is why you are writing it. Who is it directed to? How will it benefit the reader? What will they find in the pages?

Here is an example from the introduction of my last book, *A Woman Without A Man.*

This is about women. Single women who are also perhaps mothers, friends, credit card jugglers, car-poolers, entrepreneurs, lovers, workers, gardeners, even grandmothers. In short—a person trying to be everything to everybody and still have a life. I know there are some serenely, happily coupled women out there who do all the same things, and if you are one of them, I don't want to exclude you. You never know when you might need a reference guide to what it's really like out there as a single woman. And - male readers? Sure. Come along. It wouldn't hurt for you to learn something about how women really think.

If you will notice it says right away what the book is about. And in general, who it is directed towards. Use this as a guide when you write your introduction. You may discard your first copy of your introduction later since this is not your final draft. This is to refine your purpose in writing your book. This is for you to get your head around what you will be writing. Remember, do not over edit this. You will do that later.

In general, if you are not writing an epic like *War and Peace*, a book will contain approximately 200 pages. Whether it is a novel or a memoir or a self-help book. A book longer than that is not as easily saleable. But, if you have a lot to say, this is only a suggestion.

That usually breaks down to about 20 chapters with about ten pages in a chapter. That doesn't sound so ominous, does it? I suggest you make a tentative list of what each chapter will contain. But this is not written in stone either. The introduction is your guide. Next, after that first strict rule about the introduction, you have a lot of leeway. The book does not have to follow a prescribed sequence while you are writing.

Take the movies, for example. I was surprised when I found out that they did not shoot a movie in order starting from the first scene and ending with the finale. They shoot almost anywhere in the script and are mostly governed by the location of the scene. It is cheaper to do it that way. You have the cameras right there. So, you could literally write the last chapter next. Then, skip to the middle. Remember you are the architect. At the end, you will go over the whole thing and put it in the sequence that makes sense just as if you were editing a movie. And you do not have to write a complete chapter at one time.

My experience is that the "muse" shows up at odd times. When you are taking a shower, waiting for a long red light to change or on hold for the cable company. Or even if you wake at night. Just make sure that you always have a pad and pen handy so you can write down your thoughts. I guarantee if you wait until later, they will have disappeared.

Put all these pieces of paper with your latest brilliant thought in an expandable manila folder. You could label each one according to the chapter you think it might fit in later but it is an inexact science. Just write down the fragments.

Write stories about what has happened today. Especially, if they are unusual or funny. They will plump out your book. Or even be a springboard for a whole chapter.

CHAPTER TWO – WHAT IF YOUR BOOK IS A NOVEL

Writing a novel is not much different. Your "introduction" will be for you and will be the story you are telling.

Who are the characters? What do they look like? How old are they?

Where do they live? What is their connection to each other?

What is the start of the book and how do they end up?

What happens to them along the way?

It is more of an outline. A rough sketch. A storyboard.

Some people use 3x5 cards and outline the story on them. You can move them around easily.

Writing a whole book can feel overwhelming. That's why you are saying it takes time. We all have little pieces of time that we waste every day. Use them. You are a writer. You told me that. Write. A quote attributed to Goethe says it all –

What you can do, or dream you can do, begin it;
Boldness has genius, power and magic in it.

CHAPTER THREE – GREAT IDEA BUT NEED HELP?

I am not only a writer but a "ghost writer" and an editor. I have helped people write books and have done a great deal of editing of manuscripts and resumes.

This is the difference.

If you want to write a book and you think your idea has merit but you are not confident as a writer, you might consider hiring a ghost writer. This is not writing with someone whose name is also on your book. It is your book.

This is a paid person who writes as a "work for hire." They will charge by the hour, including personal conversations with you and/or by the page. Projects can take six months or more, depending on the length of the work.

You could use this person to get you started or for the whole book.

Even if you end up on Oprah and make millions, they generally do not get paid any more than was originally contracted.

Most famous people hire ghost writers for parts or all of their books. Usually this financial arrangement is negotiated by the publisher who has a contract with the writer.

For the rest of us, there are many ghost writers listed on the Internet. Do your research. It would be convenient if they lived in your area so that you could meet with them periodically to discuss how it is going but much can be accomplished by telephone or email.

Talk to them first. See if you like the person. And give them a general idea of what your book is about. Some people worry about their idea being stolen, which is not likely.

If that concerns you, you can register a rough outline, giving details about the story with the Writers Guild of America – West. Go to their site for their guidelines at www.wga.org. Note that you cannot register a name or an idea. It has to be something that is written. They suggest that it should be at least two pages of copy.

That will give you protection without going to the trouble of copywriting which is usually done after a work is finished. The cost is small and is good for five years which will stop you from worrying. You will get a registration certificate with a number. Tell the person you hire what number has been assigned to you for your work. Ghost writers do not want to wrangle with the powerful WGA.

The WGAw says the following. The work-in-progress is what I want you to notice.

Even if you have copyright through the Library of Congress, registering with the WGAw Registry creates a separate legal record for your material. In addition, you may consider registering treatments or drafts of your work-in-progress with our Registry prior to registering your final draft with the Copyright Office.

You should ask a ghost writer for several samples of their writing and see if their style coincides with the way you feel your book should sound. You want to find your "voice" in theirs. Perhaps, someone who writes like you talk. There is usually no fee for this initial contact.

Then, make sure that they have some background with your topic. You don't want a technical writer if you are composing a romantic novel.

You do have to give them something to start with. If only the outline, or what is referred to before as a "storyboard."

So much for ghost writing.

More likely, what you will need after you make some headway on your book is an editor. And, when it is finished, possibly a "book-doctor."

An editor will check all your grammar and your punctuation and most will tighten up what you have written.

A common problem with most new writers is they do not know when to stop a sentence. By the time they are done, you have lost track of what they started out to say in the first place. They are masters of the semi-colon. Everything is grammatically correct but very hard to read.

I have seen sentences that go on for a full paragraph that need to be chopped into ten different sentences. And, probably should be several paragraphs.

Steve from http://www.WriteABookNow.com, is generous with advice. He summed things up recently with this comment. "No sentence longer than 11 words, no paragraph longer than seven lines, write in the past tense always" Thanks, Steve. I always enjoy your newsletter.

If you get nothing else from this article, remember short sentences and lots of white space is good. It makes your writing easier to read and keeps the readers interest.

That is the most common service I do for writers. It may involve some re-writing but you are using their material.

Lastly, there are people who are "Book Doctors." You might consider bringing one of these in after you are completely finished with your book.

I used a book doctor on my last book. What she did is read the whole book and gave her recommendations on where things should be shifted around in sequence.

For example, I put poems in my books. She took one poem from the middle and suggested I put it at the end. She eliminated a couple. She called my attention to areas of my story which she thought should be more fully explored and expanded. Everything she told me made perfect sense.

It is hard to critique your own work. It's like trying to find a typo that someone else can spot in a second. Book doctors usually do not rewrite, They analyze your book and make suggestions. Good ones are relatively expensive. She was worth every penny. I sold the book.

N.B. You might be surprised to hear that we never feel we are finished! As your book is going to press, you will find yourself saying, "Wait a minute. I just want to change one thing." Don't bother. Everyone does that. You can do better in your next book.

CHAPTER FOUR – FINDING AN AGENT

The famous director, Billy Wilder, was a featured speaker when my son was attending USC Cinema in California.

After the presentation, he asked if he could walk him to his car.

Chattering all the way, he finally blurted out, "What is your advice about my becoming a director?"

"Do you have a relative in the business?"

"No."

""Forget it."

The days when eager, new English major graduates from Smith and Wellesley were hired by publishers to plow through piles of unsolicited manuscripts are over.

Publishers no longer accept unsolicited manuscripts. (Unless you have a relative in the business)

They only work with agents they know and trust will not waste their time. Agents who know what they can sell.

You have to find an agent to represent you. This is not easy but it can be done if you do your homework to find an agent who handles your topic.

Writers Digest is one place to start. It is published yearly and contains information on who accepts what and how to submit. You can also read this in the library.

Another source is the National Writer Union. This involves joining – pretty reasonable - and it will give you access to their web page and information on agents and everything you ever wanted to know about publishing. They also hold classes in different cities on contracts and negotiation. Worthwhile investment.

Zero in on several agents who handle books like yours and write them a dynamite query letter. Include your "platform" (read that "fans") on how you can publicize your book. Mention your connections with groups, any speaking you have done and stats on a successful blog you author. Offer to send them a few chapters of your book.

Then wait. They do not answer quickly. Write a few more letters to other agents.

You will get rejections. Don't be discouraged. It does not mean your book has no merit. It means they don't have a customer for it. If anyone responds asking for a "reading fee," ignore it. Reliable agents do not ask for money.

Be wary also of the Vanity Presses who will charge you a fortune, do nothing much to help you – and you will end up with 2500 unsold books in your basement.

The main reason you want a publisher to print your book is their DISTRIBUTION SYSTEM - to get your book in stores. Most distributors will not be bothered if you have only one book.

You might also forget any fantasies about glamorous book tours. Unless you are someone like Wayne Dyer, publishers will spend little money on you. Forget the Carrie Bradshaw episodes from *Sex and the City* when she was promoting her book with fancy parties. By the way, her "platform" in that series was her newspaper column.

If your book is accepted by a publisher, they will expect you to do almost all your own publicity.

You may decide to publish your own book. There is something about the thrill of holding a book with your name on it. It is the greatest high.

Or will you be happy with your book in a digital format like Kindle?

There are many self publishing programs. Some of the good ones are Createspace, which is affiliated with Amazon and Lulu. A few of my author friends have used them with excellent results. Shop around and see which appeals to you. They are "print-on-demand" so you don't have to put a lot of cash out. You pay by the book.

The advantage of self-publishing is you keep the money you make and do not share it with an agent. The disadvantage is again, distribution to book stores.

Amazon owns Createspace for publishing paperback book and Kindle, which is taking off like a ROCKET and outselling paperbacks with their digital design books. They sold <u>one million Kindles a week</u> in December 2011.

They operate like two different companies. And they are almost FREE.

If you want to publish a paperback book, make a new email you will only use with them and sign it with it to https://www.Createspace.com.

The advantage is that you can have them print your book and order copies as you sell. Do your research and pay attention to the format they require to print your book.

For publishing on Kindle - if you already have an Amazon account which you have used to buy books or merchandise, sign in with your regular account and scroll down to the bottom to access Kindle information. Or you can go directly to their webpage which is https://kdp.amazon.com/ They will ask you to sign in with your regular Amazon account information.

It looks as though Amazon is taking over the world of publishing now. I am using both Createspace and Kindle to publish my books and their service is excellent.

The programs require some technical ability. That is not me as I have admitted often. But after a time and many mistakes (which they excuse) you will figure it out.

If I can do it – you can. There are many manuals on it and their websites are very informative.

Once you get the hang of the two different systems, you will become a publishing genius. Almost. When they turn down your manuscript, they let you look at what you submitted so you can go back to your original word copy and fix it. And since it is all automated, there is no one to tell you how stupid you are. Nice feature.

CHAPTER FIVE –WHY NOT START WITH A MEMOIR?

Solemn faces on a tintype.

Children starched in a row.

His hand rests upon her shoulder.

Ancestors from long ago.

Was there passion in that couple?

Did they fight? Did she cry?

Did their world lay smashed around them

when that child she's holding died?

Family pictures.

Serious people.

A faded letter in a drawer.

Fragile papers tell no stories.

when the faces live no more.

I wish I knew more about my grandparents.

They arrived in April 1909 at Ellis Island from Trinidad, West Indies, with six children under ten on a ship called *Suriname*. My grandmother, Hortense, was 29. I know that much. Henry, my grandfather was 45. By the time I was five, they were both gone.

Why did they come to the harsh winters in New York from a tropical paradise? I have heard a few stories and have seen some old pictures but there is no back story. No real story.

You have a story. You have learning from your life. Things that could benefit someone.

Your grandchildren would like to know you long after you have gone.

Is it time for you to write it down?

Perhaps your book or memoir will hit #1 on the New York Times best seller list. If so, wonderful. You will make millions.

But you have something to say. It is time to say it. If not for the glory, to leave your memories behind.

Again, start anywhere. You can put it all together later. An added benefit is that you will review your life and you will remember all the wonderful memories. And perhaps exorcize the events you want to leave behind.

One day, your grandchildren or your great grandchildren will wonder about you. What your life was like – how you felt about it – who you really are. Where they came from. What were your dreams? More than just pictures from long ago in a drawer.

Will you leave them the answers? Don't leave your grandchildren and future great grandchildren wondering. Give them the back story. Your story.

CHAPTER SIX - YOU'LL GET REJECTIONS

I got my first rejection from a publisher today.

I was very proud.

Because in order to be rejected,
someone had read my work.

A professional.

And, if someone had read my work,
I must now be a writer.

One thing confused me.

I had smeared my life guts on those pages.
The ink was blood.

And the letter I received today -
said they were not accepting fiction
at this time.

CHAPTER SEVEN - YEA! A PUBLISHING DEAL

Congratulations. You have a publishing offer.

Before we pop open the champagne. One question.

Is this publisher asking in advance for some real money?
Like for production costs?

If so, you do not have a publisher. You have a Vanity Press.

Run.

Yes, they will deliver you promises and will send books.
Maybe 2500 of them. They will sit in your basement until the
day you die. You will start hoping for a small flood.

You might sell some. If you are very aggressive in
promoting. But you probably won't retrieve your investment.

A real publisher will give you money. It's called an advance.
Probably about a dollar for every book they anticipate they
will sell.

After you pay back the money advance through sales, you
will start earning a commission for every book sold. Varies,
but let's say about half of the price. Your agent gets a small
cut of this too.

So, let's presume you have a real publisher.

The first call will be a verbal offer. Then they will send a
contract.

You are going to tell me -

These people are soooooooooooooooo sweet. They LOVE my
book.

I believe in love.

THIS IS BUSINESS.

Please don't think I am raining on your parade here. Just a few suggestions for you to think and inquire about. In a nice way of course. Because they are so sweet.

Because I didn't.

I am hoping you have an agent. The boilerplate small print on the contract will make you go blind.

I happen to sell my last book myself through a contact. (Unlikely, but it can happen) I also happened to have an agent. A good one.

Shipped that hot potato right to her. She gets a percentage but worth her weight in knowledge.

There were still things we missed. But a lot we caught.

Here are a few.

HOW IMPORTANT IS THE NAME OF YOUR BOOK TO YOU?

We missed this one.

Of course they would not change it. It was such a great title. But it happened to be in the contract.

They changed it. I could not convince them otherwise.

My title was *A Woman Without A Man*. Catchy, huh?

They changed it to *Reflections from a Woman Alone*. Blah. They thought my title would offend gay people. What? I got scores of emails and letters from gay people. They loved it. They all said the same thing. The book was about relationships.

Even with their title, the biggest lesbian bookstore in Chicago would not let me present there. It was too heterosexual. They did stock it but no talk.

HOW LONG DO THEY HAVE PUBLISHING RIGHTS? You always own the copyright but when can you have it back? Make sure that is clear.

WHAT ABOUT FILM AND TV RIGHTS? Don't give these away.

Yes, I know you are writing on the sex life of the tsetse fly. It is not Steven Spielberg's thing.

But film companies are known to buy the rights of a whole book if they want one scene from it. Now, they will probably take your work and make it into a cowboy movie set on Mars but you want the right to sell it.

HOW MANY FREE BOOKS WILL THEY GIVE YOU WHEN YOUR BOOK COMES OUT?

I know. You think all those relatives will buy your book. They won't. They think they have rights to a free autographed copy. If you ask in advance you might get 50 free ones for your own use. Ask.

HOW MUCH IS THEIR BUDGET FOR PUBLICITY? You will want to go the *Book Expo* and perhaps have an allowance for travel to TV shows or book signings. Negotiate this in advance. You won't get much but you will get nothing unless you ask.

WILL THEY SEND OUT REQUESTED REVIEW COPIES ON THEIR DIME OR WILL YOU HAVE TO PAY? This used to be a given. Publicity budgets are tight. Get clear on this.

IF YOU WANT TO BUY YOUR OWN BOOK, WHAT WILL THEY CHARGE YOU FOR COPIES? You'll run out of your freebies fast. You may need more for publicity you are doing yourself. Or God forbid have more relatives and friends ask. Like your mother's best friend. Can't you give her a book?

WILL THERE BE A "GALLEY" COPY AVAILABLE FIRST? A galley is a cheap little paper book which is the preamble to the actual book. It is used to get some advance buzz going with reviewers, media and the like.

IF SO, CAN I HAVE A SUPPLY? You might want to start a little buzz of your own.

WHEN IS THE ANTICIPATED PUBLICATION DATE? Usually, unless you have a current affairs book it could be six months to a year.

You want to know this in case you have a substantial amount of money to invest in your own –

PUBLICIST

You'll need time to do research on what publicist handles your type of book. That's where their contacts are for media and print. You'll want to get costs and interview a few. They start work well before the publication date to get you listed in many possible outlets like libraries and review sites and TV and radio shows. Their deadlines are earlier than the publication date.

Whether you go this way depends on how much publicity support your publisher will give you. These days not much. The romantic book tours and cocktail receptions are mostly a thing of the past. Unless you are already a bestselling author.

ARE YOU STILL WITH ME?

I hope so because this is going to be the most exciting hairpin rollercoaster ride of your life.

A WORD OF WARNING. You will never be completely satisfied with the book. No one ever is.

When you finally have it in your hand in all its glory –

YOU WILL BE IN LOVE WITH YOUR PUBLISHED BOOK.

IT WILL BE WORTH IT. I PROMISE.

CHAPTER EIGHT – I TOLD YOU SO. YOU ARE IN LOVE.

It's right here in your hand.

You can't put it down. Read it over and over. Sleep with it on your nightstand so you can see it first thing in the morning.

An honest to God book and your name is on it. And with all lack of modesty, it is Good.

At last, you can relax. The book is printed and is on Amazon. Now to wait for the sales.

YOU HAVE GOT TO BE KIDDING

Now the work starts. Yes, STARTS.

Unless you have lots of money for a paid publicist – you are it. You have got to get it out there so your new baby can get the attention it deserves.

Do you have a blog? A webpage? If you haven't already done this – that's your first step.

If you need have help on this, Andrew Rondeau is a good resource. Check out his blog at

http://www.webuildyourblog.com

Do you have a Facebook and Twitter and Linkedin account?

This book does not attempt to be a primer on any of the above. There is much information available on line to guide you how to use them.

As long as you don't overdo it, you can promote on these social networks. (the general rule is to promote others about five to one promotion of your own)

On my own blog, I usually include an excerpt of my book before asking anyone to buy it or referring them to a source.

Second step. Get it in the hands of every friend and even those you hardly know. Contact all your blogger friends. You want them to read it and go to Amazon and/or Barnes and Noble and give a glowing review. People actually read these when they are deciding to read a book.

10 reviews are nice. 30 fabulous.

If you can't afford to buy a lot of books and send them out by snail mail, at least send a pdf. file. Then, beg a lot. Call in all your markers. All the people you have helped in the past. Don't forget promises to them in the future.

It would be nice if they also reviewed your book on their own blog.

Are you getting the picture? You are no longer a writer. Plan on at least six months to promote your book.

YOU ARE IN BUSINESS

CHAPTER NINE – MORE PUBLICITY IDEAS

Write an article based on your book and send it to your local newspaper. Find out in advance how many words are ideal for them. If they have a slow news day they might just plug it in.

Advertise in <u>RTIR</u>. It is a magazine that goes to thousands of media outlets. Not really cheap but I got many interviews out of it. I started with three months.

Getting on national or cable TV or a major radio station show is more of a challenge. But use any contacts you have and you may get lucky. Have a professional looking press kit to send out with a head shot.

Find out who the decision maker is and write directly to that person. Get the spelling and their title right. Snail Priority Mail is still used. Don't waste money on FedEx. No one will be impressed.

Speak. Speak. Speak. Bookstores are a given. But – according to the relevance of your topic – what about Rotary, Lions, University clubs, Senior Centers? These unpaid and overworked program chairpeople are always looking for speakers.

They will usually let you sell your book because you are speaking for free. Get a friend to help you handle "back of the room" sales.

Don't overlook Public Access Television in your town. Start looking at the local shows and approach producers who look like they might have interest in your topic.

Internet radio, like ***Blog Talk Radio***, is a great way to get publicity. There are quite a few now. Again, do your research and listen to some of the shows to see who features topics like yours. Contact them individually by name and make reference to the shows you have heard. No mass emails please. You don't want to contact a sports show if your subject is archeology. Offer to send them a copy of your book on request.

If they don't answer, contact them again. Mention you are available on short notice. Some guests cancel late.

TV and radio shows are voracious monsters. They need to be fed constantly with new guests. So don't be shy. Keep asking. You are doing them a favor by filling their space.

Start your own show on one of the Internet radio stations. Most are free and will allow you to promote your own products. Ask your talented friends to come on and interview you. Then return the favor. Everyone is selling something these days.

Interview other people on your own show. You can also plug your own book along the way. For tips on how to do an interview, see the next chapter. Remember Larry King?

One of the advantages of the Internet radio stations is they usually allow you to post the show to your blog. So it keeps on giving even if you don't have a lot of audience at first. People can listen later.

Pay to be interviewed. Michelle Vandepas offers a great publicity program on her site http://www.talkingbooksTV.com. She will do a ten minute interview and since she is a super tech, will then blast it all over the Internet. For a couple.of hundred dollars, you can get great coverage. You can also put that interview on Amazon as a comment and use it on your own site.

CHAPTER TEN – INTERVIEW LIKE LARRY KING –
Learning from the pro

After 400 shows as a producer/host on national cable for
Wisdom Television, I learned a thing or two.

Who was my media coach? You guessed it. Larry King.
Watched him every night. Still miss his program.

Here are a few things I learned.

1. This is probably the most important point that Larry made.
Your guest is the star of the show. Not you. Do not give your
opinion on anything. Do not tell stories about your
experiences. Nobody cares.

2. Research. Research. Research. Pretend your guest has
asked for a big loan. Check out everything about them. Make
a list of all possible questions. Give your guest the list and
have them add to yours. Give them the probable first
question.

3. Short intro. No more than two minutes. I always liked to
start with a question. Like "Are you wondering what to do
about —-? (whatever) We have help for you today. " You
want to engage your listener right away. Then, a few
credentials. Do not mention why you asked them to be on
your show. That's about you. This interview is about them.
Thank them warmly for coming on.

4. Listen. I know you have YOUR LIST of questions you
have prepared. But if your guest says something provocative,
stop and ask about it.

I swear I have heard some interviewers who if their guest
said, "I just drowned my cat," instead of saying, "WHAT???"
would go on to their next question. This is a conversation, not
an interrogation.

5. Assume your audience knows nothing. So start with the basics. For example, I once had an author on my TV show who was a Buddhist nun. She was surprised when I told her my first question was "Who was Buddha?" She said everyone knew. They don't.

6. Ask a question once. Don't add a tail on it like, "In your book you refer to ——Can you explain it? I mean that is quite a statement. Where did you get that idea?"
Let the first question hang out there. Your guest got the question the first time.

One of my favorite questions Larry King asks is just "Why?"

Another one is "What happened?"

7. Don't interrupt.. Unless your guest is hijacking your show with self-promotion. Then interrupt and bring them back to explore an earlier point in the interview. Tell them in advance you will promote them. They don't have to do it.

8. No personal questions. Unless you clear it with your guest first.

9. Avoid technical terms. See #5.

10. At the end of the interview, be sure to thank your guest for taking the time to come on your show.

11. Recap their bio briefly at the close – "We have been talking to -etc.

12. Don't promote yourself until the very end. You are entitled to a short promo but make it real and appropriate and short. Something like – "*You have been listening to (Name of Your Show) with (Your Name) the author of (Your Book) For more information on my book, please check out my website at (Your blog or Website)*

CHAPTER ELEVEN – SOMEONE WANTS TO INTERVIEW YOU ON RADIO

EXCITEMENT!

You have a request for an interview.

When I was doing interviews for *Wisdom Television*, I was like a dog with a bone. I not only read every book of every author, I dug into all their other books, read all the reviews. I knew more about them than their own mothers.

I thought every interviewer did that.

Now I had a book to sell. And I was in for a shock.

I got a lot of requests for interviews from RTIR. Not small stations. Big ones in New York and San Francisco – all over the country. They were done by phone.

Only a few had looked at my press kit and almost no one had opened the book. I had even included some questions they could ask me to help them.

I think most of these people did not know who they were interviewing until a few minutes before the show.

The first question was invariably this –

"So, what's your book about?"

WHAT?

I realized I had to design my own interview to get the ball rolling. What some people call a "thirty second.elevator pitch."

You have to give enough information about your book so that the interviewer had some fodder to ask follow up questions.

My book was called *A Woman Without A Man.*. Here's an example of how I answered.

"My book, A Woman Without A Man *is a book about a young widow facing life as a single. But it is not a book about grief. It is a book about entering society that you have not experienced for years."*

And all the rules of being single have changed.

That gives the interviewer an entrance to at least ask "How?"

I would answer – (GOD! There is a whole half hour to fill up with this person)

To give them an idea and use up time I would read them the prologue of the book. It is a poem that would give them some understanding.

You only get a minute.

The stone has not been set

before you get the question

"Are you seeing someone yet?"

You have not filed the insurance,

transferred a single bond

before they sing the litany

"Remember, life goes on."

It's not the lonely evenings

that strike terror in your breast.

It's the envelopes that come addressed

to "Ms. You and your guest."

The dilemmas' not in grieving

or even what to wear

but where you find a body

to escort you to affairs.

They say you're far too fussy.

There is nothing much out there.

They use as their criteria

if a man can breathe and stare.

I'd run away to Tonga,

Abu Dhabi or Tibet,

but I know that someone there would ask

"Are you seeing someone yet?"

If you find yourself a widow,

start wailing right away.

You only get a minute

before you have to play.

That gives the interviewer an opening to ask more questions.

I am not going to go through an entire interview with you but just to give you an idea of how you have to actually take control of the interview.

You probably have some stories in your book. Tell them.

You can turn almost any odd question over with something like, *"That reminds me of something in my book that was (interesting – funny-informative – you choose)*

You can't do this off the cuff. You actually have to make a script for yourself and practice and practice – maybe with a friend who can feed you questions.

It's almost like designing a speech. In segments.

Be sure to bring up the title of the book several times in the interview. Just casually

Then end with a promo for yourself. Especially if you can see you are not going to get it from this interviewer.

"It was really fun being with you today. I hope your audience will be interested in knowing how to get my book, A Woman Without A Man." Then tell them.

Be sure to be gracious and thank the person, by name, for having you on.

That's the framework. Does it sound shameless?

It is.

Can you do it? Sure you can.

CHAPTER TWELVE – OH- OH – A VIDEO INTERVIEW

WHY ARE YOU SCARED?

YOU LOOK TERRIBLE.

You don't look terrible. You look like you.

Try a little experiment. Next time you get on public transportation, look carefully at the faces sharing the bus or train.

How many of them are beautiful? Study them. Just ordinary looking people. Many are probably very nice but I want you to concentrate on the faces.

Those are the same kind of faces who will be looking at your video. They are not judging you by the way you look.

THEY WANT TO HEAR WHAT YOU HAVE TO SAY

When I first started to do a TV show, I had to do an opening to introduce the guest. I had done my share of public speaking – but I was talking to people – eyes – reactions – smiles. An audience.

I found it difficult to talk into a camera. Nobody there. Just the lens.

So I took a course with a drama coach. It was a training for students who were interested in getting jobs doing commercials. Same problem. They were talking to nobody too.

HE GAVE US A FEW VALUABLE TIPS:

He agreed that it was hard to talk into a camera.

HE SAID TO GET A CLEAR PICTURE IN YOUR MIND OF A PERSON YOU LOVE VERY MUCH.

PUT THE PICTURE IN THE CAMERA LENS.

THEN TALK TO THAT PERSON.

It changes everything.

Let's take a look at a few other things.

MAKEUP

Yes, you will look better with a little. Get some pancake type with a sponge. You dudes too. We all have some flaws we could touch up to even out our complexion.

Don't neglect your eyes– people look mostly at your eyes when you talk. Men don't know to do eyes subtly. Get a girl friend to outline that area. Make you pop a little on the screen.

WHAT YOU WEAR

A friend and I rented a booth at the big TV convention in Las Vegas. OK. It was a card table in the back with two chairs and a TV set that played a loop of some of my shows. You could spot us on the way to the rest rooms.

A young man stopped for a minute. He introduced himself as a stylist from Hollywood.

"Lose the blouse and jacket. Wear a loose sweater in a color that flatters you. People pay thousands for my advice and this is free."

Done from that moment. Besides, it's comfortable.

LIGHTING

You will probably be on a webcam at your end.

Tricky at first. You'll have to experiment so you are not in the dark or so hot that you burn eyes.

Maybe you can sit near a window that gives you some light. Be inventive. You can try some construction lights that clip on somewhere and point to the ceiling. Get some at Home Depot. They are reasonable. Move a few lamps from another room. Experiment. It's not rocket science and no one is expecting studio quality.

BACKGROUND.

One sentence. Get rid of the mess behind the shot. It's distracting.

THE FOLLOWING TIPS WILL GUARANTEE YOU DO THE WORST POSSIBLE INTERVIEW:

1. Don't be nervous. It is not natural.

2. Don't listen to the interviews that have already been done by the host. You want to be as spontaneous as possible, right?

3. Don't take out your book or product and look at it objectively.

4. Don't decide what are the most interesting or unique parts.

5. Ignore your primary message. Let your host figure it out. They asked you.

6. Assume your host has done serious homework and knows all about you.

7. Don't send in a list of the questions you would like to be asked.

8. Make sure the answers can be answered with a simple yes or a no. You want to drive the interviewer crazy.

8. Don't practice answering the questions you have listed. No, not in your head. Out loud. Maybe in a mirror.

9. Talk very slowly. People can take a little nap while you are speaking.

10. Don't pull out a few short stories to spice up your points.

11. Always promote yourself and your product as often as possible during the interview. Keep spelling out your URL This is about you anyway.

12. Wear a crazy print or a T shirt with a slogan on it. Maybe a baseball cap would be more effective.

13.. Be prepared to never be invited back again by anyone.

14. To insure this, put the bad interview on your webpage or blog.

MOST IMPORTANT

15. Ignore all these tips and be your own charming self.

Especially #1– It is OK to be nervous. It gives you an edge. The famous actress, Helen Hayes, said she would never want to get on a stage with an actor who did not have stage fright.

You love your readers, don't you? Now love the interviewer.

Get into the conversation with your interviewer as though you are chatting with an old friend.

CONCLUSION – COMMUNICATION

The old man was sitting with his hat on the sidewalk. He had a sign.

HELP! HUNGRY.

Very few people stopped. A marketing executive did.

He took the sign, turned it around, and changed it. It now read –

HELP!

HAVE YOU EVER BEEN HUNGRY?

People stopped and threw a few coins in the hat frequently after the change. WHY?

THE COMMUNICATION WAS DIFFERENT.

It was personal.

I had an interview with Michael Ray Dresser who has a show on *BlogTalk Radio* called *Dresser After Dark.* He's been on radio for 27 years.

The topic was my book, *A Woman Without A Man.* It was a good interview. He is a pro.

He has an offer to all of his guests. After the interview, he will give you free evaluation.

Figured. What the heck. Why not take him up on it? I can always learn something new.

He had a suggestion on how I could have improved the interview. The story above about the sign is Michael Ray Dresser's story.

He asked whether a single woman was a threat to married women. Was it different at a party if you did not have a partner?

I said yes and then added – A lot of single women have told me the same thing.

Then came the AHA moment.

Why didn't you say that in the interview?

I don't know. Why?

Because you missed an opportunity to communicate with all the single women who were listening. You did not include them.

Such a small thing. But, so important. Communication. He was right.

My sign should have read –

HELP!   ARE YOU SINGLE TOO?

WHAT DOES YOUR SIGN SAY?

SAY IT.

ABOUT THE AUTHOR

Corinne Edwards has traveled several life paths - from business owner to sales trainer, author, lecturer, poet, TV producer, blogger and media coach.

She is the author of *Low Pain Threshold, Love Waits on Welcome, Reflections from a Woman Alone, A Woman Without A Man, Sales, Lies and Naked Truths* and *When Your Husband Has Died – A Survival Guide.*

She produced/hosted *Book Tours.., with Corinne Edwards* for *Wisdom Television* on national cable. She does media coaching for others now.

In recent years, her focus has shifted to the area of personal growth and human potential. Corinne has conducted self esteem classes based on the principals of *A Course in Miracles* in Cook County Jail. Her program for rehabilitation for prostitutes was one of the first of its kind in the country.

Currently, her passion is blogging on her site http://www.personal-growth-with-corinne-edwards.com. She can be reached at miraclecor@aol.com.

DISCLAIMER

Any resources mentioned in this book are strictly for information purposes to the reader and do not produce income to the author. All of the resources mentioned have been used personally by the author.

www.ingramcontent.com/pod-product-compliance
Lightning Source LLC
Chambersburg PA
CBHW070237290526

45789CB00004B/1662